KB244207

The World's Most Astonishing Festivals

About Wise & Wide

- A systematic 6-level English reading program based on Lexile® measures
- Diverse and interesting topics chosen from the elementary curriculums of Korea and English speaking western countries
- Well-written books in various forms including fiction stories, descriptive texts, and classics retold
- The informative but original fiction stories grab your interest, leading to the easy and clear understanding of the educational content.
- Improve thinking skills with solid after-reading activities at all levels of the series.

Wise & Wide is a 6-level English reading program that consists of 60 books and each level is systematically divided by Lexile® measures. The Lexile® Framework for Reading is the most popular reading measuring system in American formal education curriculums and many English programs. Over 20 out of 50 states in the U.S. mark Lexile® measures directly on students' final report cards and over 300 well-known publishers adopt and use Lexile® measures.

Experience many kinds of readings written by professional writers from the U.S. and England. They used interesting topics that were carefully chosen after analyzing elementary curriculums from around the world including Korea, the U.S., England, and Australia among many others. Comprehensive after-reading activities including graphic organizers, speaking tasks, and After-reading Tests are ready for you.

Levels in the series and their corresponding Lexile® measures

Level	Lexile® measures	U.S. Grade
Level 1	Below 200L	Pre K - K
Level 2	190L - 400L	Lower Grade 1
Level 3	350L - 530L	Upper Grade 1
Level 4	420L - 650L	Grade 2
Level 5	520L - 940L	Grade 3 - 4
Level 6	830L - 1070L	Grade 5 - 6

* Smart Readers: Wise & Wide level 1 is applicable to the preschool level in the U.S.

* The source of the relationship between Lexile® measures and U.S. school grades: CCSS(Common Core State Standards) FOR ENGLISH LANGUAGE ARTS, APPENDIX A (2012, which is used by 45 states in the U.S.)

Topic List

	Level 1	Level 2	Level 3	Level 4	Level 5	Level 6
Book 1	Science>Biology: The hibernation of animals Story	Science>Biology: Living and nonliving things Story	Science>Biology> Animals & the Environment: Sea otters Story	Environment> Living with nature: The diver & the persimmon tree Story	Science>Biology> Animal: Amazing animals of the Amazon Story	Science>Biology: Germs, transmitted diseases Story
Book 2	Literature> World classics: Aesop's fables Story	Literature> Traditional fairy tale: Old tales about stones Story	Social Studies> Economy: To run a business to make and save money Story	Science>Biology> Plants: Photosynthesis Story	Science>Earth science: Earth's layers,earthquakes, volcanoes, and earth's atmosphere Report	Mathematics> Sequence: The golden ratio & the Fibonacci sequence Story
Book 3	Science>Physics: How shadows are formed Story	Literature> World classics: Peter Pan Story	Science>Scientific technology: Nanobots Story	Literature>Myths: World's creation stories Story	Literature> Legend: The story of King Arthur Story	Literature>Myths: Constellation myths Story
Book 4	Literature> Traditional literature: The Talmud Story	Science>Biology> Animal: Polar bears Story	Science>Biology> Animal: Mountain gorillas Story	Social Studies> Cultural anthropology: Amazing ancient cultures of the world Story	Science> Earth science: Clouds and weather Story	Literature> Human & animals: The friendship between a girl and a horse Story
Book 5	Social Studies> Ethics: Rules in daily life Story	Science>Biology: The five senses Report	Social Studies> Cultural anthropology: Astonishing festivals Report	Art>Music: Stories from two operas Story	Social Studies> World culture & history: The Renaissance Story	
Book 6	Social Studies> World geography & travel: Tourist attractions around the world Story	Science>Biology> Animal: Dinosaurs Story	Science> Astronomy: The solar system Story	Social Studies> People: Three great people who overcame hardships Story	Science>Scientific technology: The wonderful world of robots Report	
Book 7		Social Studies> Cultural anthropology: Mythological monsters from around the world Report		Science & Social Studies> Technology & culture: Inventions from around the world Report	Art>Works of art: Famous paintings Report	
Book 8				Social Studies> History: the California Gold Rush Report	Social Studies & Science> Psychology: Psychology in everyday life Story	
Book 9						
Book 10						

10 books in each level will be published.

How to Use This Book

•Before Reading

You can easily find the topic and what kind of story you are about to read.

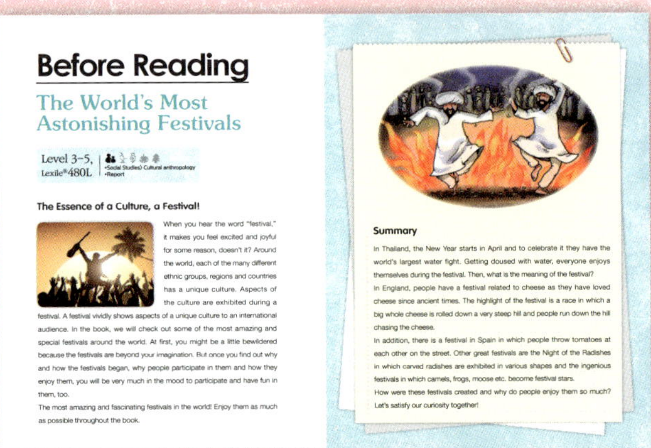

•The text

All the stories were written by professional writers from the U.S. and England, so you will read authentic and appropriate English sentences and expressions in every book in the series.

•Pop Quiz

Check out right away if you understand what you have just read by solving a pop quiz that checks your comprehension.

•Key Words

The key words and expressions on each page are listed for you to easily study them.

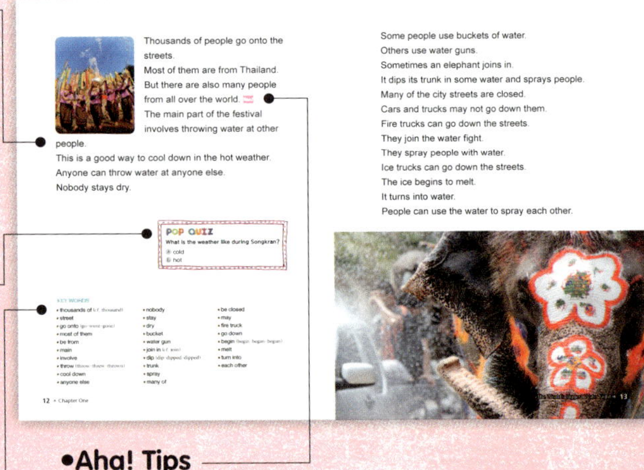

•Aha! Tips

Download free Korean explanations at *www.ihappyhouse.co.kr* for all of the sentences marked with "Aha!". These explain cultural, scientific, and economic knowledge or they deal with aspects of English such as grammatical structures or idiomatic expressions. There are lots of "Aha! Tips" to help you understand the text.

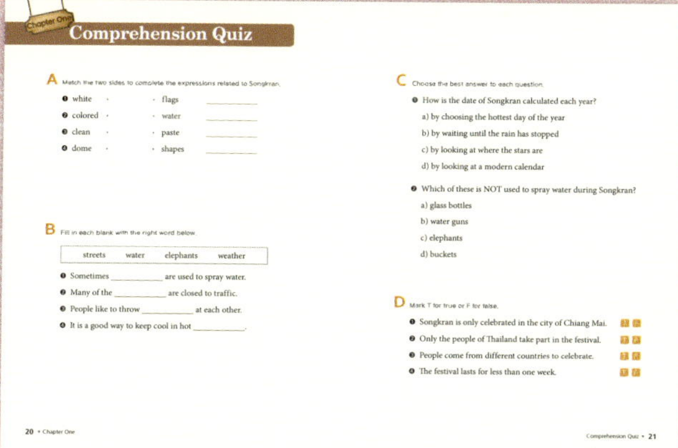

•Comprehension Quiz

After reading one chapter, solve various questions to find out if you fully understand the content.

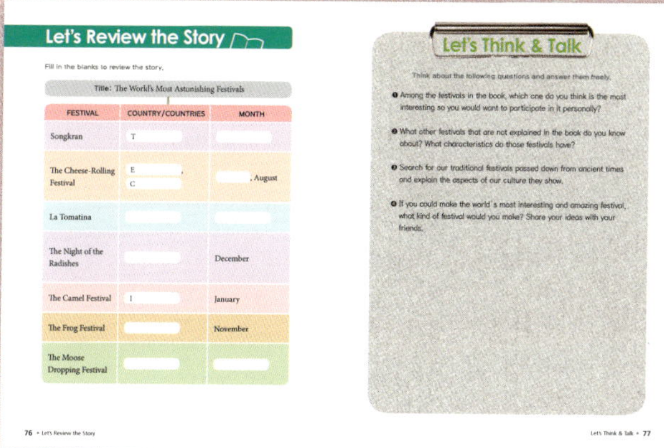

•Let's Review the Story /
•Let's Think & Talk

Fill in the blanks in the organizer to summarize the whole story. Express your own thinking and feelings about the story by answering the questions. You can build up logic and reasoning skills for your essay examinations in the future.

Appendix

Audio CD

In the CD audio book form, the texts are read vividly by American professional voice actors.

After-reading Test

Solve an additionally provided After-reading Test for each book.

The Korean translation, Answer Keys, a Word Quiz, a Word List, and Aha! Tips for each book

You can download them for free at *www.ihappyhouse.co.kr*

Before Reading

The World's Most Astonishing Festivals

Level 3-5,
Lexile® 480L

•Social Studies)Cultural anthropology
•Report

The Essence of a Culture, a Festival!

When you hear the word "festival," it makes you feel excited and joyful for some reason, doesn't it? Around the world, each of the many different ethnic groups, regions and countries has a unique culture. Aspects of the culture are exhibited during a festival. A festival vividly shows aspects of a unique culture to an international audience. In the book, we will check out some of the most amazing and special festivals around the world. At first, you might be a little bewildered because the festivals are beyond your imagination. But once you find out why and how the festivals began, why people participate in them and how they enjoy them, you will be very much in the mood to participate and have fun in them, too.

The most amazing and fascinating festivals in the world! Enjoy them as much as possible throughout the book.

Summary

In Thailand, the New Year starts in April and to celebrate it they have the world's largest water fight. Getting doused with water, everyone enjoys themselves during the festival. Then, what is the meaning of the festival?

In England, people have a festival related to cheese as they have loved cheese since ancient times. The highlight of the festival is a race in which a big whole cheese is rolled down a very steep hill and people run down the hill chasing the cheese.

In addition, there is a festival in Spain in which people throw tomatoes at each other on the street. Other great festivals are the Night of the Radishes in which carved radishes are exhibited in various shapes and the ingenious festivals in which camels, frogs, moose etc. become festival stars.

How were these festivals created and why do people enjoy them so much?

Let's satisfy our curiosity together!

Contents

The World's Most Astonishing Festivals

The World's Most Astonishing Festivals

The World's Biggest Water Fight

KEY WORDS

- biggest
- fight
- festival
- take place
- April
- hottest
- dry season (↔ rainy season)
- both A and B
- traditional
- calendar
- modern
- be calculated by
- position
- celebrate
- all over
- last

▲ New Year anniversary festival at Chiang Mai

In Thailand, there is a festival called the Songkran Festival. **Aha!** It takes place in April every year.
This is the hottest time of the year in Thailand.
It is the end of the dry season.
The people of Thailand have both a traditional calendar and a modern one.
April is their traditional New Year.
The date is calculated by the position of the stars.
People celebrate all over Thailand.
But the biggest Songkran Festival takes place in the city of Chiang Mai.
It lasts for six days.

▲ Thailand

Thousands of people go onto the streets.

Most of them are from Thailand.

But there are also many people from all over the world.

The main part of the festival involves throwing water at other people.

This is a good way to cool down in the hot weather.

Anyone can throw water at anyone else.

Nobody stays dry.

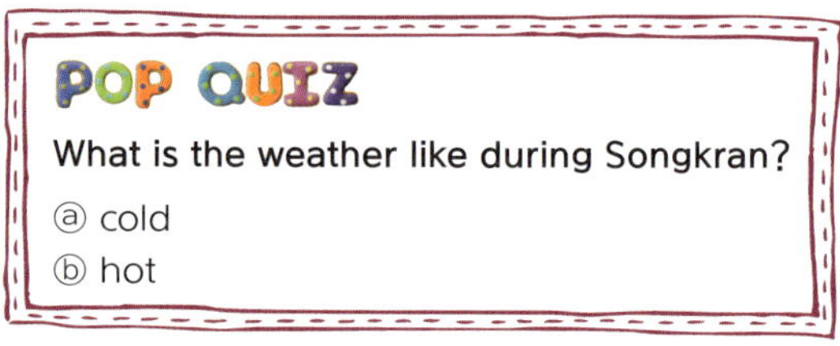

KEY WORDS

- **thousands of** (*cf.* thousand)
- **street**
- **go onto** (go-went-gone)
- **most of them**
- **be from**
- **main**
- **involve**
- **throw** (throw-threw-thrown)
- **cool down**
- **anyone else**
- **nobody**
- **stay**
- **dry**
- **bucket**
- **water gun**
- **join in** (*cf.* join)
- **dip** (dip-dipped-dipped)
- **trunk**
- **spray**
- **many of**
- **be closed**
- **may**
- **fire truck**
- **go down**
- **begin** (begin-began-begun)
- **melt**
- **turn into**
- **each other**

Some people use buckets of water.

Others use water guns.

Sometimes an elephant joins in.

It dips its trunk in some water and sprays people.

Many of the city streets are closed.

Cars and trucks may not go down them.

Fire trucks can go down the streets.

They join the water fight.

They spray people with water.

Ice trucks can go down the streets.

The ice begins to melt.

It turns into water.

People can use the water to spray each other.

There are some rules in order to keep people safe.

Police stand by the gates where people go into the festival.

They make sure that nobody takes in glass.

They make sure that nobody takes in weapons.

They make sure that there is nothing that could hurt anyone.

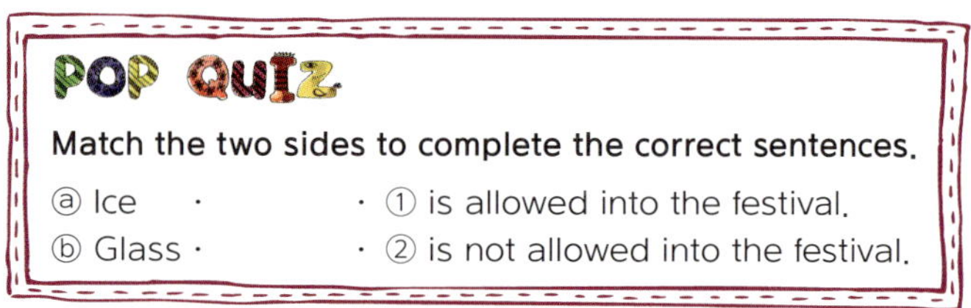

KEY WORDS

- rule
- in order to + *Verb*
- keep someone safe (keep-kept-kept)
- stand (stand-stood-stood)
- by the gate

- make sure
- take in (take-took-taken)
- weapon
- hurt (hurt-hurt-hurt)

But the Songkran Festival is not just about throwing water.

It is a time for visiting relatives and friends. **Aha!**

It is a time for visiting older people and showing them respect.

Songkran is also a festival for followers of the Buddhist religion.

They go to Buddhist monasteries.

These are special places where they pray.

Some people have a statue of Buddha in their homes.

They wash it with clean water.

The water has some perfume in it to make it smell fresh.

The people hope they will have good luck all year.

Sometimes people clean their entire houses.

The new year is a new start for them.

They decide to try to behave well all year.

Some Buddhists take sand
to a monastery.
They think about the dirt on
their feet.
They carry some away
each time they leave the
monastery.
So, at Songkran, they bring
some back to replace it.
The sand at the monastery
is made into dome shapes.
It is decorated with colored
flags. **Aha!**

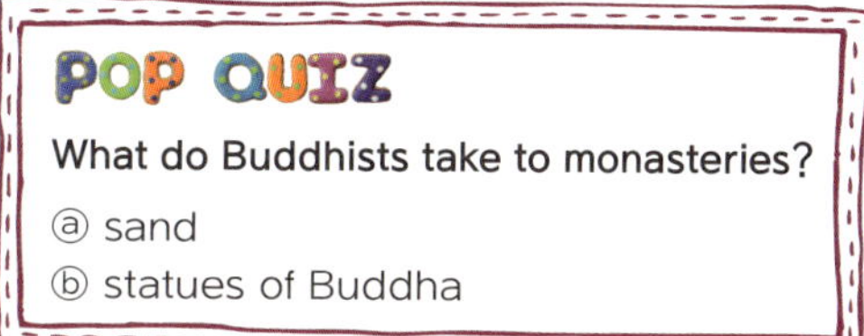

KEY WORDS

- statue
- perfume
- **make** (make-made-made)
- smell
- fresh
- good luck
- all year
- entire
- decide

- try to + *Verb*
- behave well
- dirt
- carry away
- each time
- **leave** (leave-left-left)
- bring back
  (bring-brought-brought)
- replace

- dome
- be made into
- be decorated with
  (*cf.* decorate)
- colored
- flag

But why do the people of Thailand throw water at each other during Songkran?

It is a type of blessing.

It is a way to give good luck to other people.

Sometimes they mix chalk into the water.

It makes a white paste.

They put it on people's faces and bodies.

This is another form of blessing.

The water fight is also a sign that people want to get rid of the bad things in their lives.
They wash the bad away and promise to do good things instead.
But most of all, it is a great way to cool down.

Comprehension Quiz

A Match the two sides to complete the expressions related to Songkran.

❶ white   •   • flags   _____________

❷ colored •   • water   _____________

❸ clean   •   • paste   _____________

❹ dome   •   • shapes   _____________

B Fill in each blank with the right word below.

streets	water	elephants	weather

❶ Sometimes _____________ are used to spray water.

❷ Many of the _____________ are closed to traffic.

❸ People like to throw _____________ at each other.

❹ It is a good way to keep cool in hot _____________.

 Choose the best answer to each question.

❶ How is the date of Songkran calculated each year?

a) by choosing the hottest day of the year

b) by waiting until the rain has stopped

c) by looking at where the stars are

d) by looking at a modern calendar

❷ Which of these is NOT used to spray water during Songkran?

a) glass bottles

b) water guns

c) elephants

d) buckets

D Mark T for true or F for false.

❶ Songkran is only celebrated in the city of Chiang Mai.   T   F

❷ Only the people of Thailand take part in the festival.   T   F

❸ People come from different countries to celebrate.   T   F

❹ The festival lasts for less than one week.   T   F

The Cheese-Rolling Festival

In England, lots of people like cheese. 

They like to eat it and to cook with it.

But there is one place where they do something different.

This festival is so dangerous that the police warn people not to do it each year.

But still, at the end of May, thousands of people gather from all over the world.

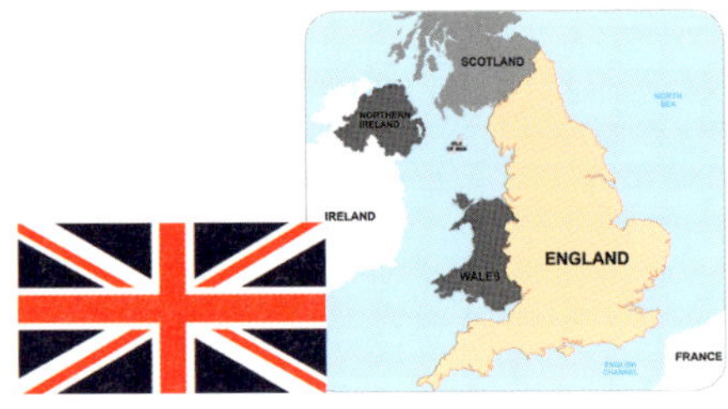

▲ England

- roll
- lots of (= a lot of)
- different
- dangerous
- warn
- each year
- at the end of
- gather

▲ A whole cheese is big and round.

They meet at a place called Cooper's Hill.

It is a very, very steep hill.

It is so steep that you cannot run down it without falling over. **Aha!**

- **meet** (meet-met-met)
- **hill**
- **steep**
- **run down** (run-ran-run)
- **without** (↔ with)
- **fall over** (fall-fell-fallen)

Most of the people stand on the hill to watch.

But some people line up at the top.

They want to have a race down the steep hill.

But this is no ordinary race.

The people are not just racing against each other.

They are racing against cheese!

When people eat cheese, they usually eat just a little bit.

But a whole cheese is big and round.

It weighs three or four kilograms.

KEY WORDS

- line up
- at the top
- have a race (have-had-had)
- ordinary
- race (against)
- usually
- just a little bit
- whole
- weigh

- heavy
- mean (mean-meant-meant)
- run after
- catch (catch-caught-caught)
- reach
- bottom
- too
- for
- this is why

To begin the race, a whole cheese is rolled down the
hill.

The hill is very steep, and the cheese is very heavy.

This means that the cheese rolls very fast.

All of the people in the race run after the cheese.

They try to catch it before it reaches the bottom of the
hill.

But the cheese goes too fast for them.

So all of the people fall over!

This is why the event is dangerous.

Often, people get badly hurt.

Ambulances have to stay nearby in order to take them to hospital.

Some people get cuts and bruises.

Others break their arms or their legs.

Sometimes they injure their backs.

If someone cannot walk, a fire crew sets up a system of ropes.

They carefully lift the injured runner onto a stretcher.

They pull the runner to the top of the hill so that he or she can be loaded into an ambulance. **Aha!**

The police watch the race, too.

They make sure that everybody behaves well.

Sometimes the rolling cheese hits someone in the crowd.

The cheese is very heavy.

It can knock a person over and hurt that person badly.

Some years, plastic cheese is used instead.

The plastic cheese is safer than the real cheese.

But it does not roll as well.

KEY WORDS

- often
- get hurt
- badly
- ambulance
- nearby
- cut
- bruise
- break one's arm (break-broke-broken)
- injure
- back
- set up (set-set-set)

- a system of ropes (*cf.* system)
- lift
- injured
- runner
- stretcher
- pull
- load into
- hit (hit-hit-hit)
- in the crowd
- knock over
- safer

There are four downhill races against the cheese.

Then, at the end of the day, the children have their own race.

But they run up the hill without any cheese.

This is more tiring than running down the hill.

But it is much safer.

The children do not fall over.

They do not hurt themselves.

KEY WORDS

- downhill (↔ uphill)
- own
- run up

- tiring
- much

There is one winner for each race.
The prize is the cheese.
It is the same one that rolled down
the hill.
You might think that the cheese
would be broken after all of that
rolling.
But it is protected by a wooden
case and decorated with ribbons.
When the plastic cheese is rolled,
the winner gets a real one instead.
The prize for the children's race is
usually a smaller cheese.

POP QUIZ

Where might the children start their race?

ⓐ at the bottom of the hill
ⓑ at the top of the hill

KEY WORDS

- winner
- each race
- prize
- might
- be broken
- protect
- wooden
- smaller

Why do the people at Cooper's Hill have a cheese-rolling festival?

It has been going on for two hundred years.

Even before that, people rolled things down the hill.

They tied up thin branches of wood.

They set fire to the branches.

Then, they rolled the branches down the hill.

They did it to celebrate when winter was over.

They were happy that spring had come.

They were happy that their crops would grow again.

KEY WORDS

- have a festival
- have been + *Verb*-ing
- go on
- tie up
- thin

- branch
- set fire to
- be over
- crop
- **grow** (grow-grew-grown)

A similar festival takes place in Whistler, Canada, in the month of August. (Aha!)
At Whistler, there are more prizes for the races.
As well as the cheese, winners get a ski pass.

▲ skiers enjoying skiing in Whistler, Canada

Children win T-shirts for their races.
The Canadian event is much safer than the one in England.
Contestants wear helmets and kneepads.
The hill is less steep.

▲ Canada

KEY WORDS

- in the month of August
- as well as
- ski pass
- win (win-won-won)
- contestant
- kneepad
- less

There are different cheese-rolling events, too.

In cheese bowling, cheese is rolled through an
obstacle course.

It is difficult and requires some skill.

Some people do not want to race.

Instead, they can taste different cheeses.

Children can have their faces painted.

If they want, they can learn about how cheese is made.

And, of course, they can buy plenty of cheese to take
home.

- bowling
- through
- obstacle course

- require
- skill
- of course

- plenty of

Comprehension Quiz

A Which of these injuries can you get if you race against the cheese on Cooper's Hill? Choose all the correct answers.

cuts

bruises

burns

stings

loose teeth

broken arms

B Mark T for true or F for false.

❶ Police and fire fighters race each other to catch the cheese. T F

❷ To begin the race, the people start before the cheese. T F

❸ Ambulances take injured people to the top of the hill. T F

❹ The rolling cheese weighs up to 4 kg. T F

C Choose the best answer to each question.

  ❶ Which race happens at the end of the day?   CHILDREN/ADULTS

  ❷ Which race is run uphill?   CHILDREN/ADULTS

  ❸ Which race is run against the cheese?   CHILDREN/ADULTS

D Complete the table to compare the two different cheese festivals. Use the words provided.

T-shirts	bowling	helmets
cheese	ambulances	ski pass

	COOPER'S HILL	WHISTLER
Country	England	Canada
Prize	__________ ❶	cheese and a __________ ❷
Children's Prize	cheese	__________ ❸
Safety Precautions	__________ ❹ attend to take people to the hospital.	Runners wear __________ ❺ and kneepads.
Other Races	none	cheese __________ ❻

The Tomato-Throwing Festival

This festival happens in Spain in the town of Bunol. **Aha!**

It takes place every year on the last Wednesday of August.

This is in the middle of summer, when the weather is very hot.

▲ Spain

KEY WORDS

- happen
- in the middle of
- take part in
- get in
- the name of

People come from all over the world to take part in the festival.

Sometimes, fifty thousand people come.

There are too many people for such a small town.

So each person must buy a ticket to go to the festival.

Only twenty thousand people can get in.

This makes it safer for everyone.

The name of this festival is La Tomatina.

But many people call it "The World's Biggest Food Fight."

The festival lasts for a week.

There is music and dancing.

People join a parade on the streets.

Fireworks light up the sky at night.

On Tuesday night, there is a cooking contest.

The people cook paella. **Aha!**

This is a Spanish dish containing rice.

There is also seafood in it and sometimes meat.

▲ paella

▲ gazpacho

▲ jamón

▲ churros

On Wednesday morning, the tomatoes arrive.

Trucks bring tons and tons of tomatoes.

The people gather in the center of town.

Some of them wear gloves to protect their skin. **Aha!**

Some of them wear goggles to protect their eyes.

Tomato juice can sting.

KEY WORDS

- parade
- firework
- light up
- cooking contest
- paella
- Spanish
- dish
- contain

- seafood
- arrive
- tons and tons of
- center of town
- glove
- goggles
- **sting** (sting-stung-stung)

To begin the festival, someone must climb up a wooden pole.

There is a ham at the top of it.

The pole is as high as a two-story house. **Aha!**

It is covered with grease, so it is difficult to climb.

If someone reaches the ham, this is a signal.

The festival can begin.

If nobody reaches the ham, a different signal is needed.

Water cannons are fired into the crowd instead.

At last, the tomato throwing can begin.

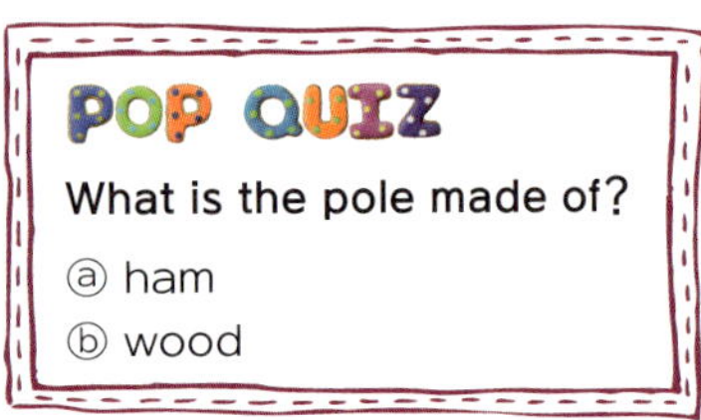

KEY WORDS

- climb up
- wooden pole
- at the top of
- two-story house
- be covered with[in]
- grease
- signal
- be needed
- water cannon
- be fired into
- at last

Everyone throws tomatoes at each other.

There are tomatoes everywhere.

The streets are full of tomatoes.

The people are covered in tomatoes.

Their skin turns red.

They are practically swimming in tomato juice!

But there are some important rules.

People must follow them.

Then, they will be safe and not get hurt.

1. People must not bring bottles or other hard objects.

   If they throw hard things, people can get hurt.

2. People must not rip each other's clothes.

3. People must squash the tomatoes before they throw them.

4. People must not go too close to the trucks.

After one hour, water cannons are fired again.

This means the tomato throwing must stop.

Fire trucks drive through the streets.

They spray water on the streets to wash them.

Tomato juice is an acid. 

This means it cleans the streets very well.

They are left very clean.

The fire trucks do not wash the people.

They must go to the river to wash themselves.

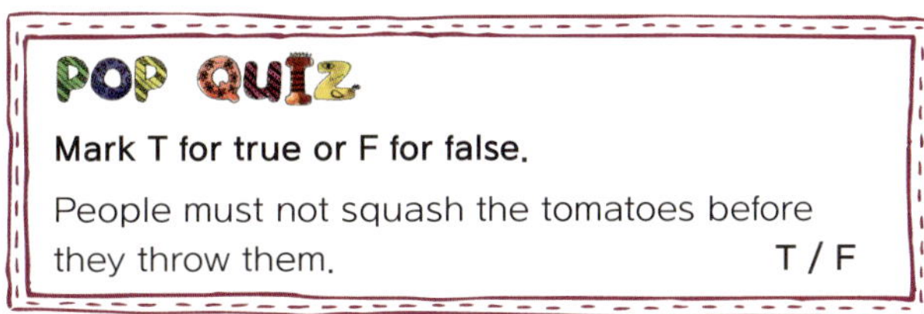

KEY WORDS

- follow
- hard
- object
- rip
- squash

- drive through (drive-drove-driven)
- spray
- acid
- be left + *adjective*

Why do the people of Bunol have such a festival?

It began around seventy years ago.

Nobody knows how it began.

Some people have different ideas.

1. Some friends had a food fight.

   Other people thought it looked fun.

   So they joined the fight.

2. Some people threw tomatoes at a bad musician.

   They did not like his music.

3. A truck was carrying tomatoes through the town.

   The tomatoes spilled onto the ground.

   People picked them up and began to throw them.

4. The people of the town were cross with the town leaders.

   So they threw tomatoes at them.

However it began, people enjoyed it.

So they decided to do it again each year.

Comprehension Quiz

A Match the two sides to make pairs of words that are similar in meaning.

❶ rip •   • a) injured

❷ close •   • b) near

❸ hurt •   • c) begin

❹ start •   • d) tear

B Circle the right word for each underlined part.

❶ (People / Tomatoes / Goggles) gather in the center of the (paella / town / festival).

❷ (Tomatoes / Bottles / Gloves) must not be (thrown / cleaned / covered) at other people.

❷ (Fireworks / Cannons / Trucks) bring the (acid / water / tomatoes) into town.

❹ People (squash / tip / wash) themselves in the (truck / river / paella).

C Choose the best answer to each question.

❶ Why can't everybody go into the town for the tomato-throwing festival?

a) There aren't enough tomatoes.

b) The town is small.

c) Only Spanish people are allowed in.

d) They are too busy making paella.

❷ Which of these is NOT a possible reason for why the tomato-throwing festival began?

a) Some people thought a food fight looked fun.

b) Some people tried to clean the streets with tomatoes.

c) Some people threw tomatoes at the town leaders.

d) Some people played with the tomatoes that spilled from a truck.

D The following sentences are about the process of the tomato-throwing festival. Put the sentences in order.

❶ Everyone starts to throw tomatoes at each other.

❷ Fire trucks spray water on the streets.

❸ Someone climbs the pole and tries to reach the ham.

❹ The streets and the people get covered in tomato juice.

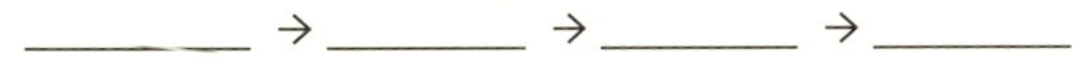

_______ → _______ → _______ → _______

The Night of the Radishes

Mexico is known for its colorful festivals. 

On December 23 each year, thousands of people go to the city of Oaxaca.

They gather for the Night of the Radishes.

This may sound like the title of a horror film, but it is an amazing contest.

People have to carve amazing shapes out of radishes.

▲ Mexico

KEY WORDS

- radish
- be known for
- colorful
- Oaxaca
- horror film
- carve

A radish is a root vegetable.

It is red on the outside and white on the inside.

It has a strong flavor.

It is good to eat.

Ordinary radishes are quite small.

▲ radishes

But special radishes are grown for the contest.

They are much bigger than ordinary radishes.

One radish may weigh three kilograms.

It may be up to fifty centimetres long.

The radishes are left in the ground for a long time.

This helps them to grow big.

It also makes them grow into strange shapes.

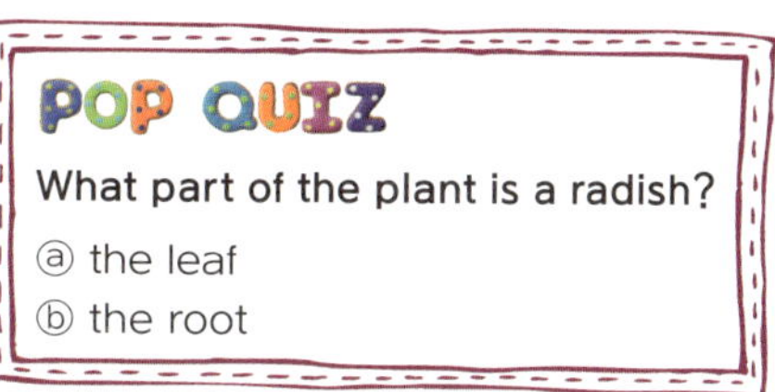

KEY WORDS

- outside (↔ inside)
- flavor
- quite

- up to
- for a long time

They are dug out of the ground on December 18.

They are delivered to people who want to carve them.

The people have a few days to do their work.

They carve the radishes into amazing shapes.

They can be people or animals.

They can be buildings or trees.

Lots of radishes are put together to form a scene. **Aha!**

It might be a scene from history.

It might be a scene from a religion.

It might be a scene from city life.

There are radishes shaped like cats and dogs.

There are radishes shaped like bugs and snakes.

There are babies and children as well as men and women.

Some of them wear dresses carved with flowers and stars.

Some of them are tiny.

Some of them are taller than you.

- **dig out of** (dig-dug-dug)
- **deliver**
- **put together**
- **a scene from**
- shaped like
- bug
- tiny

Thousands of people go to look at all of the radishes.

But only one radish can be the winner.

The winning radish must be unique.

That means it is different than all the rest.

It must also show the most skill in carving.

The carver of the winning radish has his or her photograph taken.

It appears in the city newspaper.

The winner also gets a prize of more than 1,000 U.S. dollars.

KEY WORDS

- look at
- winning
- unique
- different than
- the rest
- most
- carver
- have one's photograph taken
- appear
- continue

The radish-carving contest lasts for one night.

But people celebrate for two more days.

The festival continues on Christmas Eve and

Christmas Day.

There are music, dancing, and a street parade.

There are fireworks for everyone to watch.

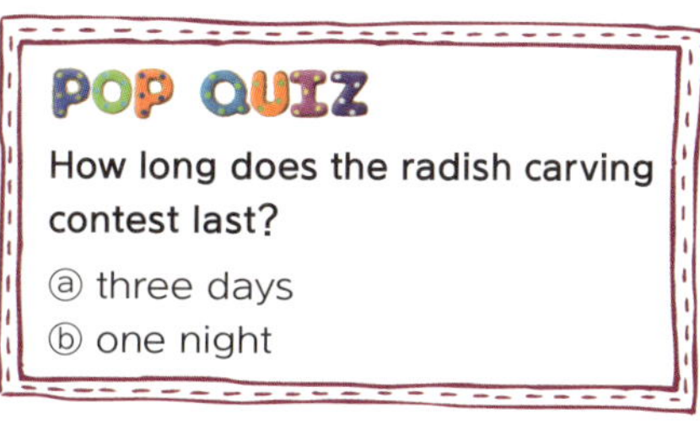

Why do the people of Oaxaca have a radish-carving
contest?

Around five hundred years ago, Spanish people
brought radishes to Mexico.

The people of Mexico had never seen radishes before. Aha!

They did not know what they were.

Some farmers wanted to sell the food they grew.

They had a stall.

They wanted people to come and to buy things.

So they carved radishes into special shapes.

They put the radishes on their stalls.

People came to the stalls to see the carved radishes.

Then, they bought lots of food.

KEY WORDS

- **farmer**
- **sell** (sell-sold-sold)
- **stall**
- **buy** (buy-bought-bought)

Chapter Four

Comprehension Quiz

A Fill in each blank with the right word below.

| stalls | buy | celebrate | carved |

❶ Some of them wear dresses __________ with flowers.

❷ People __________ for two more days.

❸ The farmers set up __________ to sell their radishes.

❹ They wanted people to come and to __________ their radishes.

B Mark T for true or F for false.

❶ There are several winners in the contest.   T F

❷ The winner gets a prize of $100.   T F

❸ The winner is the person who takes
the best photograph.   T F

❹ The winner must be very good at carving.   T F

 Choose the best answer to each question.

❶ What must people do to take part in the contest at the Night of the Radishes?

   a) They must make a horror film.

   b) They must grow the biggest radish.

   c) They must carve radishes into different shapes.

   d) They must paint radishes in different colors.

❷ Why are the radishes left in the ground for a long time? Choose two answers.

   a) to make them grow bigger

   b) to make the taste better

   c) to make them a deeper red color

   d) to make them grow into strange shapes

❸ What festival takes place immediately after the Night of the Radishes?

   a) The Day of the Radishes

   b) a film festival

   c) Christmas

   d) Easter

Various Animal Festivals

The Camel Festival

This unusual festival takes place in India. **Aha!**

There is a remote desert city called Bikaner.

Camels are very important there.

Before cars were invented, they were the main form of transport.

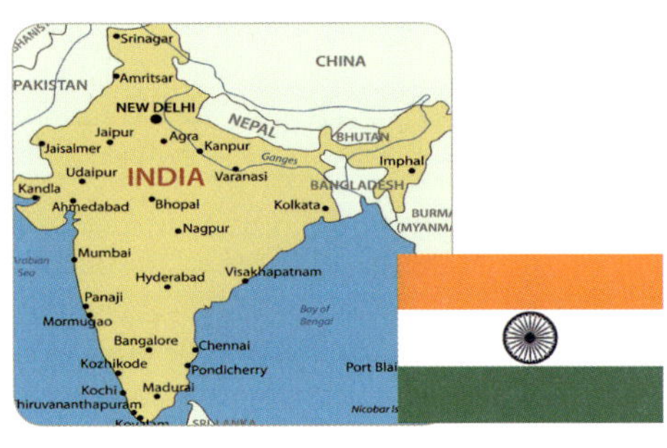

▲ Republic of India

Sometimes, camels are called "Ships of the Desert."

Each January, the people hold a camel festival.

It lasts for two days.

KEY WORDS

- camel
- unusual
- remote
- desert
- Bikaner
- transport

- hold a festival (hold-held-held)
- procession
- rider
- walk through
- richly
- saddle

- bridle
- jewel
- glitter
- jingle
- feast
- all of the senses

The festival begins with a
procession.
Camels and riders walk
through the crowd.
The camels wear richly
decorated saddles and
bridles.
There are many camel-
themed contests.
A prize is offered for the best
dressed camel.
Their jewels glitter in the sun.
Bells jingle across the sand.
It is a feast for all of the senses.

Some camels have designs cut into their fur.
There is a prize for the best design.
There is also a contest for the best camel haircut.
The camel-milking contest is popular.
Camel milk is used to make tea and sweets.
People can taste them at the festival.
Then comes the camel dancing.
The camels sway and dance gracefully.
Their drivers tell them what to do.
It is an amazing sight.

KEY WORDS

- design
- milk
- sweets
- sway
- gracefully
- second
- fastest
- region
- **compete** (*cf.* competition)

- fierce
- be considered
- honor
- local
- tourist
- in one's bare feet
- surprisingly
- seem
- harm

On the second day, the camel races take place.

The fastest camels in the region compete.

Their riders all want to win, so the competition is fierce.

It is considered a great honor to win the race.

Thousands of people — both locals and tourists — go
to watch.

On both evenings, there is singing and fire dancing.

People dance on a fire in their bare feet.

Surprisingly, it does not seem to harm them.

But this is not something you should try.

The Frog Festival

There are lots of frogs in the USA.

The best place to see them is in the town of Rayne. Every year in November, fifty thousand people arrive there.

They go to the Frog Festival.

Frogs don't mind getting wet.

But some people do.

So a huge tent is put up.

Then, if it rains, the people will stay dry.

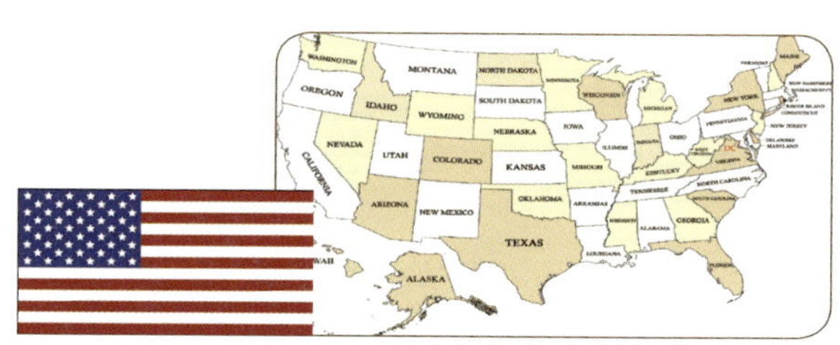

▲ USA(United States of America)

KEY WORDS

- Rayne
- mind
- get wet

- huge
- tent
- put up

▲ downtown Rayne

Lots of different things happen at the Frog Festival.

There are fairground rides for everyone.

Some of them are very fast.

Others are slower.

These are better for young children.

Some people dress up as frogs.

They listen to music, and they dance about.

Real frogs are used for special contests.

There is a frog-racing contest.

The winner is the frog that moves the fastest.

There is a frog-jumping contest.

The winner is the frog that jumps the furthest.

Anyone can take part in these contests.

If you don't have your own frog, you can rent one.

KEY WORDS

- furthest
- rent (*cf.* lend)
- have a name
- at least
- tree frog
- enter
- get squashed
- feed (feed-fed-fed)
- soybean
- once
- sit still (sit-sat-sat)

There are some rules for the frog contests.

1. Each frog must have a name.

2. Each frog must be at least ten centimeters long.

   Tiny tree frogs may not enter.

   They are too small.

   They might get squashed under people's feet.

3. Owners must not feed hot sauce to their frogs.

   That makes them jump faster.

4. Owners must not feed rice or soybeans to the other frogs.

   That makes them jump more slowly.

5. Once the race has started, owners must not touch their frogs.

   If a frog sits still, its owner may blow on it.

   The owner may shout at it.

   The owner may jump up and down.

   But the owner must not touch the frog at all.

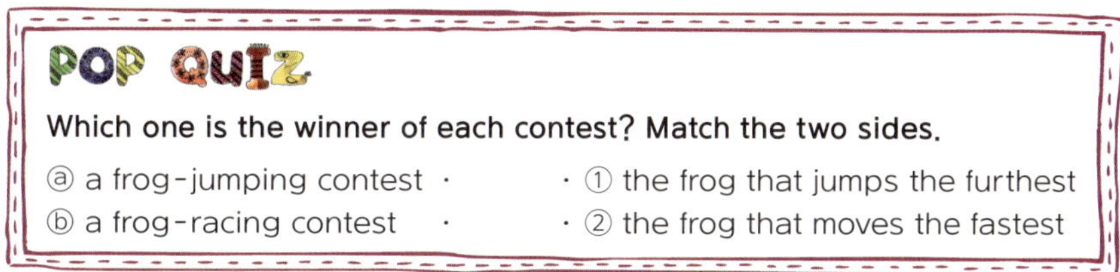

There is also a best dressed frog contest.

The owner of each frog makes a tiny outfit for his or her frog.

The owners are sometimes called jockeys.

The jockeys dress up, too.

They wear shorts and checkered shirts. **Aha!**

They also wear matching caps.

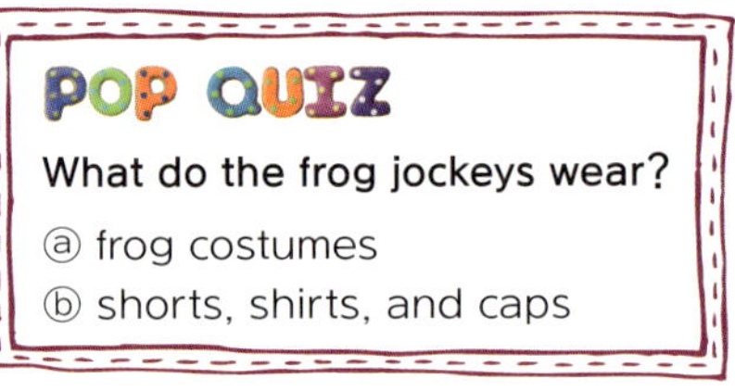

KEY WORDS

- outfit
- jockey
- shorts
- checkered
- shirt
- matching
- cap

The Moose Dropping Festival

This is perhaps the strangest festival of all.

It takes place in Alaska, USA.

This is very far north.

It is cold and snowy in the winter.

So people like to celebrate in the summer.

- moose
- dropping (*cf.* drop)
- perhaps
- strangest
- Alaska
- far
- north
- Talkeetna
- produce
- poop
- fancy
- craft
- for sale
- jewelry

In the town of Talkeetna, there is a festival each July.

It is called the Moose Dropping Festival.

A moose is a very large animal.

There are lots of moose in Alaska.

The moose produce a lot of poop.

The fancy name for poop is dropping.

So this is really the Moose Poop Festival.

At the festival, there are stalls that have crafts for sale.

There are stalls that have jewelry for sale.

All of the things are made from moose droppings.

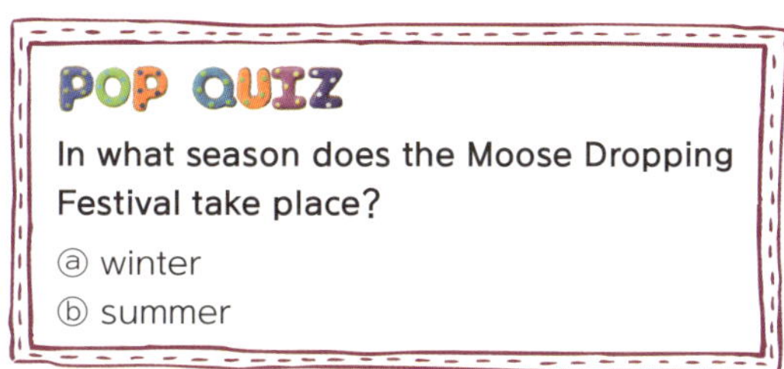

How did such a strange
festival begin?
It began in 1972.
Some boys wanted
to attract visitors to
Talkeetna.
They thought about
different ways to do it.
They went into the forest.

▲ moose droppings

They found some moose droppings there.
Each one was shaped like a small egg.
The boys baked the droppings in the oven.
Then, they painted the droppings with varnish.
This made them hard and shiny.
The boys invented a game.
First, they made a board with numbers on it.
Players had to throw the droppings onto the board.
People enjoyed playing the game.
Visitors began to come to Talkeetna.

KEY WORDS

- attract
- visitor
- bake

- varnish
- shiny
- board

VARNISH

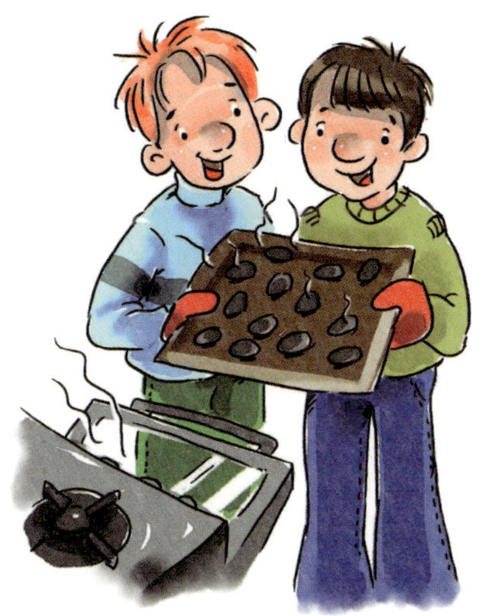

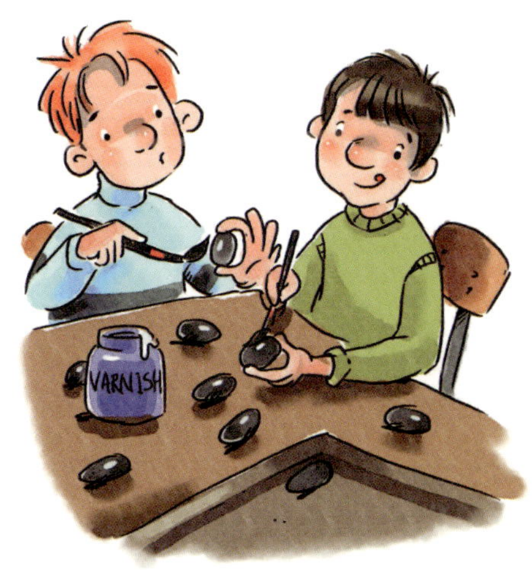

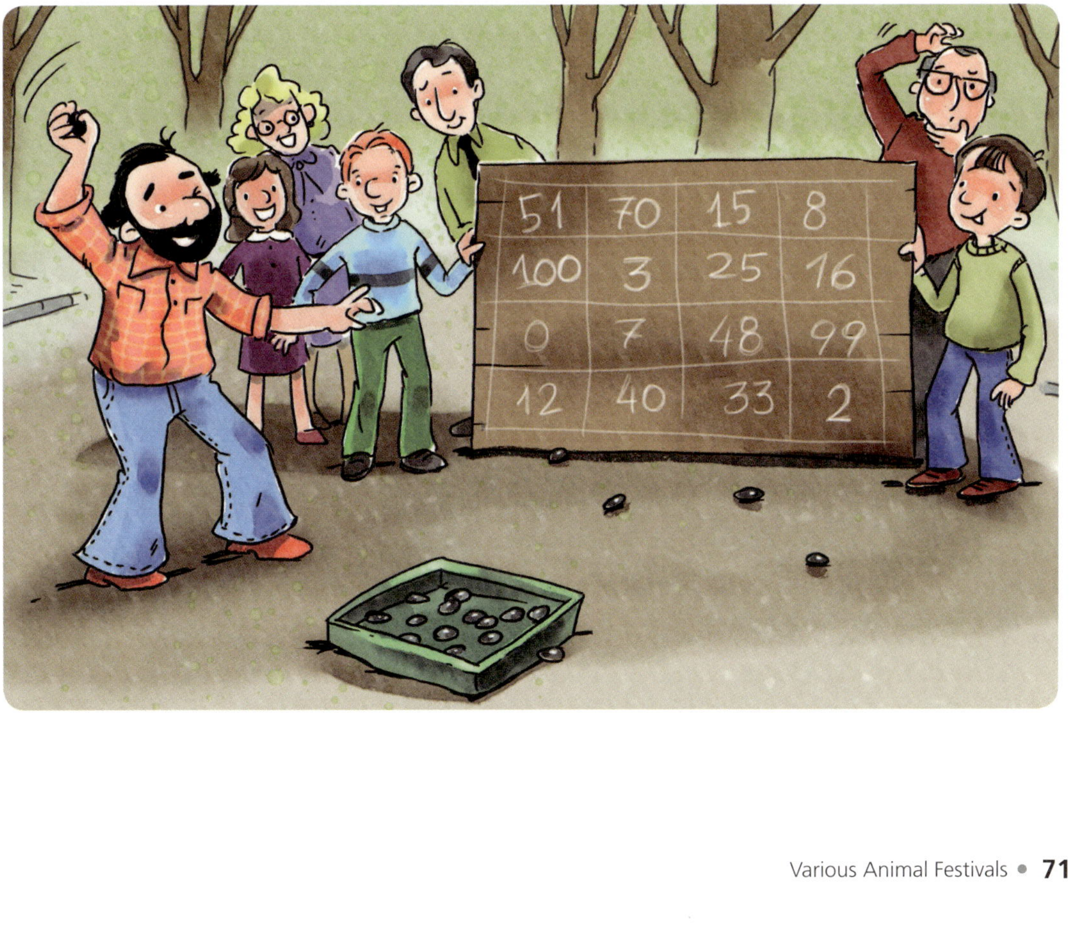
51 70 15 8
100 3 25 16
0 7 48 99
12 40 33 2

Now the game has changed.

It is much more exciting.

People go up in hot-air balloons.

They look down on the showground.

There are some targets on the ground.

The targets have numbers on them.

The people in the balloons have moose droppings.

They drop them onto the ground.

If a dropping lands on a target,

they win some money.

This strange festival
began with two boys.
They had a good idea.
All of the other festivals began in simple ways.
People wanted to celebrate or to have some fun.
Perhaps you have an idea for a festival where you live.
Who knows?
People may celebrate it for years to come.

KEY WORDS

- hot-air balloon
- showground
- target
- land
- Who knows?
- for years to come

Comprehension Quiz

A Mark T for true or F for false.

❶ A moose is a very small animal. T F

❷ There are lots of moose in Alaska. T F

❸ A moose makes a lot of poop. T F

❹ The Moose Dropping Festival began with two girls. T F

B Put the sentences in order.

❶ Two boys painted the droppings with varnish.

❷ Two boys found lots of moose droppings.

❸ Two boys went into the forest.

❹ Two boys baked the droppings in the oven.

__________ → __________ → __________ → __________

 Choose the best answer to each question.

1 If your frog sits still, which of these must you NOT do?

a) touch it

b) blow on it

c) shout at it

d) jump up and down

2 How do people stay dry at the Frog Festival?

a) They carry umbrellas.

b) They go into a tent.

c) They wear raincoats.

d) They stay at home.

3 Why are camels so important in Bikaner?

a) People eat them.

b) People worship them.

c) People hunt them.

d) People ride on them.

4 Which one is NOT true about the Bikaner Camel Festival?

a) The festival begins with a procession.

b) The camels wear richly decorated bridles.

c) The drivers dance gracefully.

d) The camels are milked in a contest.

Let's Review the Story

Fill in the blanks to review the story.

Title: The World's Most Astonishing Festivals

FESTIVAL	COUNTRY/COUNTRIES	MONTH
Songkran	T	
The Cheese-Rolling Festival	E , C	, August
La Tomatina		
The Night of the Radishes		December
The Camel Festival	I	January
The Frog Festival		November
The Moose Dropping Festival		

Let's Think & Talk

Think about the following questions and answer them freely.

❶ Among the festivals in the book, which one do you think is the most interesting so you would want to participate in it personally?

❷ What other festivals that are not explained in the book do you know about? What characteristics do those festivals have?

❸ Search for our traditional festivals passed down from ancient times and explain the aspects of our culture they show.

❹ If you could make the world's most interesting and amazing festival, what kind of festival would you make? Share your ideas with your friends.

Let's Review the Story

Title: The World's Most Astonishing Festivals		
FESTIVAL	COUNTRY/COUNTRIES	MONTH
Songkran	Thailand	April
The Cheese-Rolling Festival	England, Canada	May, August
La Tomatina	Spain	August
The Night of the Radishes	Mexico	December
The Camel Festival	India	January
The Frog Festival	USA	November
The Moose Dropping Festival	USA	July

[Photo Credit]

p.25

By Dave Farrance (Own work) [CC BY-SA 3.0 (http://creativecommons.org/licenses/
by-sa/3.0) or GFDL (http://www.gnu.org/copyleft/fdl.html)], via Wikimedia Commons

p.41

By flydime (Flickr: La Tomatina / Spain, Buñol) [CC BY-SA 2.0 (http://
creativecommons.org/licenses/by-sa/2.0)], via Wikimedia Commons

p.50

By drewleavy (Flickr) [CC BY-SA 2.0 (http://creativecommons.org/licenses/by-
sa/2.0)], via Wikimedia Commons

p.51

By AlejandroLinaresGarcia (Own work) [CC BY-SA 4.0 (http://creativecommons.org/
licenses/by-sa/4.0)], via Wikimedia Commons

p.52

By AlejandroLinaresGarcia (Own work) [CC BY-SA 4.0 (http://creativecommons.org/
licenses/by-sa/4.0)], via Wikimedia Commons

p.63

By Falkonry at English Wikipedia [Public domain], via Wikimedia Commons

p.68

By Frank K. from Anchorage, Alaska, USA [CC BY 2.0 (http://creativecommons.org/
licenses/by/2.0)], via Wikimedia Commons

p.69 left photo

By Dave Bezaire & Susi Havens-Bezaire (Flickr: Another Moose Sighting) [CC BY-
SA 2.0 (http://creativecommons.org/licenses/by-sa/2.0)], via Wikimedia Commons

∗ Others are from shutterstock.com.

Smart Readers: **Wise** & **Wide**

After-reading Test

- **The World's Most Astonishing Festivals**
- **Level 3**
- **29 Questions**

(Vocabulary 7 / Reading Comprehension 16 /

Sentence Structure & Grammar 6)

1. What does "unique" mean in the following sentence?

   The winning radish must be unique.

   ① the best   ② the biggest
   ③ not like any other ④ easy to see

2. Which of the following is a pair of words that are similar in meaning?
   ① quite – astonishing
   ② gather – jump
   ③ outside – inside
   ④ form – make

3. Which one best explains the meaning of "traditional"?
   ① with pictures
   ② in the dry season
   ③ scientific
   ④ has been done for many years

4. Which one is the closest to the meaning of "contest" in the following sentence?

   There is a frog racing contest.

   ① showground   ② competition
   ③ ride   ④ tent

5. Which one best explains the meaning of "popular"?
   ① messy   ② liked by lots of people
   ③ difficult to do ④ busy

6. What is the difference between "locals" and "tourists"?

    ① Locals can dance, but tourists can't.

    ② Locals ride camels, but tourists don't.

    ③ Locals live nearby, but tourists are just visiting.

    ④ Locals drink camel milk, but tourists don't.

7. Which of the following is NOT a pair of opposites?

    ① huge ↔ tiny

    ② fast ↔ slow

    ③ wet ↔ dry

    ④ begin ↔ bake

8. Which vehicles are allowed onto the city streets during Songkran? Choose two answers.

    ① cars   ② buses

    ③ fire trucks   ④ ice trucks

9. Why do the police stand by the gates during Songkran?

    ① so that they will not get wet

    ② so that they can go home early

    ③ so that they can make sure no glass is brought in

    ④ so that they can spray people with water

10. During Songkran, what do people promise to do?

    ① clean their houses more often

    ② visit their relatives

    ③ pray at monasteries

    ④ do good things and behave well

11. Why did the people celebrate the coming of spring?
① Their crops would grow again.
② They could go on a holiday.
③ It was time for the cheese festival.
④ Lots of visitors would arrive.

12. Why is the Whistler festival safer than the one at Cooper's Hill?
Choose two answers.
① The cheese is made of plastic.
② The runners wear protective clothing.
③ The hill is less steep.
④ The festival happens in the snow.

13. Which of these can people NOT do at the Whistler Cheese Festival?
① cheese bowling　　　　　　② cheese painting
③ cheese buying　　　　　　④ cheese tasting

14. What is cheese bowling?
① using cheese to knock down a target
② carving a bowl out of cheese
③ rolling cheese through an obstacle course
④ a contest to see who can eat the most cheese

15. Which of these is NOT part of the tomato-throwing festival?
① cooking　　　　　　② fireworks
③ sword fighting　　　　　　④ dancing

16. Which one is correct information related to the tomato-throwing festival?
  ① Paella contains rice.
  ② The tomatoes arrive by train.
  ③ There are fireworks on each morning of the festival.
  ④ People gather at the edge of the town.

17. How do the people get clean after fighting at the tomato-throwing festival?
  ① Acid is sprayed onto them.
  ② Water is sprayed onto them.
  ③ They go to the swimming pool.
  ④ They wash themselves in the river.

18. What is the difference between an ordinary radish and a radish for the contest?
  ① A contest radish cannot be eaten, but an ordinary radish can be eaten.
  ② A contest radish is much smaller than an ordinary radish.
  ③ A contest radish does not stay in the ground for as long as an ordinary radish.
  ④ A contest radish is much bigger than an ordinary radish.

19. What does the winner of the radish-carving contest receive?
  ① a newspaper   ② some money
  ③ some carving tools   ④ a big radish

20. Why did the farmers first carve their radishes?
  ① to bring themselves good luck
  ② to make people come to their stalls
  ③ to win a contest
  ④ to celebrate Christmas

21. Why must owners of frogs not feed other people's frogs?
   ① The frogs might jump more slowly.
   ② The frogs might bite.
   ③ The frogs might need special diets.
   ④ The frogs might be frightened of someone they don't know.

22. What is made from camel milk?
   ① chocolate   ② sweets
   ③ face cream   ④ paints

23. Why did the boys invent the first moose dropping game?
   ① They wanted to bring visitors to their town.
   ② They wanted to play it with their friends.
   ③ They wanted to make jewelry.
   ④ They wanted to make some money.

※ Choose the right word(s) for each blank. (24~25)

24.
It is a time for __________ relatives and friends.

   ① visited   ② to visit
   ③ visit   ④ visiting

25.
They pull the runner to the top of the hill __________ he or she can be loaded into an ambulance.

   ① so to   ② so that
   ③ that so   ④ to so

26. Choose the wrong part of the sentence.

The pole is <u>as</u> <u>high</u> <u>than</u> a <u>two-story</u> house.
　　　　　① 　② 　　③ 　　　　④

※ Choose the correct sentence. (27~29)

27. ① They are racing against cheese.
　② They will racing against cheese.
　③ They are race against cheese.
　④ They will raced against cheese.

28. ① It is so steeper than you cannot run down it without falling over.
　② It is so steep that you cannot run down it without fall over.
　③ It is so steep that you cannot run down it without falling over.
　④ It is so steeper than you cannot run down it without falls over.

29. ① Lots of radish are put together to form a scene.
　② Lots of radish is put together to form a scene.
　③ Lots of radish is put together to forms a scene.
　④ Lots of radishes are put together to form a scene.

Sarah J. Dodd
Sarah J. Dodd is an experienced primary school teacher who resides in the UK, but has also lived and taught in Australia. She has a PhD in Science and a certificate in Creative Writing. She has published several books for children: "An Angel Anyway" (Anyway Press, 2008) the "Little Angels" series (Lion Children's Books, 2009/10), "The Lion Picture Bible" (Lion Children's Books, 2015) and "Legs: the tale of a meerkat lost and found" (Lion Children's Books, 2015). Her poetry for children has also been highly commended and published in the anthology "Let in the Stars" (Manchester Metropolitan University, 2014).
She is currently working on further picture books for the very young, and a novel for older children.

The World's Most Astonishing Festivals

Written by Sarah J. Dodd
Illustrated by Nika Tchaikovskaya

First Published in October 2015

Editorial Manager: Juyon Choi
Editors: Juyon Choi, Kyunghee Jang, Jiyeong Park
Designer: Eunhee Lee
Cover Designer: Eunhee Lee

Published and distributed by

Darakwon Bldg., 64-1 Jandari-ro, Mapo-gu, Seoul, Korea 04031
Tel: 82-2-736-2031(ext. 250)   Fax: 82-2-732-2037
Homepage: www.ihappyhouse.co.kr
Publisher: Kyudo Chung

ISBN: 978-89-6653-207-0 18740 / 978-89-6653-156-1 18740(set)

[Components]
• 1 Audio CD (Recording Studio: Aram)
• Answer Keys & Korean Translation: Free download at www.ihappyhouse.co.kr